THIS BOOK BELONGS TO

13-Digit ISBN: 978-1604336252
10-Digit ISBN: 1604336260

This book may be ordered by mail from the publisher. Please include $3.95 for postage and handling. Please support your local bookseller first!

Books published by Cider Mill Press Book Publishers are available at special discounts for bulk purchases in the United States by corporations, institutions, and other organizations. For more information, please contact the publisher.

Cider Mill Press Book Publishers
"Where good books are ready for press"
12 Spring Street | PO Box 454
Kennebunkport, Maine 04046
Visit us on the Web! www.cidermillpress.com

Design by Shelby Newsted
Typography: Georgia, Academy Engraved, Gebetsbuch Initialen, Type Embellishments One

Art credits, in order of appearance:
Cover wrap image: B. Holl engraving of William Shakespeare from a print by Arnold Houbraken (Library of Congress); William Shakespeare's signature (Wikimedia Commons); front endpapers: illustrated view of London and the Globe Theatre in 1647, 1810 (Folger Shakespeare Library) and portrait of Shakespeare, 1623, by Martin Droeshout (Wikimedia Commons); decorative element on title and quotation pages: AKaiser/Shutterstock. com; quill illustration, MapcnoStudio/Shutterstock.com; border illustration in the Introduction: Roberto Castillo/Shutterstock.com; Walter Crane illustration from *Two Gentlemen of Verona* (Folger Shakespeare Library); Walter Crane illustration from *Two Gentlemen of Verona* (Folger Shakespeare Library); Walter Crane illustration from *The Tempest* (Folger Shakespeare Library); Walter Crane illustration from *Two Gentlemen of Verona* (Folger Shakespeare Library); Walter Crane illustration from *The Tempest* (Folger Shakespeare Library); Walter Crane illustration from *Two Gentlemen of Verona* (Folger Shakespeare Library); Walter Crane illustration from *Two Gentlemen of Verona* (Folger Shakespeare Library); Walter Crane illustration from *The Tempest* (Folger Shakespeare Library); Walter Crane illustration from *Two Gentlemen of Verona* (Folger Shakespeare Library); Walter Crane illustration from *The Tempest* (Folger Shakespeare Library); Walter Crane illustration from *Two Gentlemen of Verona* (Folger Shakespeare Library); back endpapers: portrait of Shakespeare, 1849, by Samuel Cousins (Library of Congress, Prints & Photographs Division, LC-USZ62-5812) and reconstruction illustration of the Globe Theatre, 1958, by C. Walter Hodges (Folger Shakespeare Library)

Printed in China
1 2 3 4 5 6 7 8 9 0
First Edition

SHAKESPEARE

NOTEBOOK

CIDER MILL
PRESS

BOOK
PUBLISHERS

Kennebunkport, Maine

Introduction

By Joelle Herr, author of *William Shakespeare: The Complete Plays in One Sitting* and *William Shakespeare Rewritten by You*

 y any standard, William Shakespeare was a very prolific writer. Though he lived to be only around fifty-two years old, he penned a whopping thirty-eight plays, 154 sonnets, and two epic (read: *long*) narrative poems—all over the course of twenty-five years. Along the way, he coined more than 1,500 words and hundreds of phrases, so many of which are still in use today. If you've ever used the words *generous, madcap, radiance, scuffle, swagger*, and *zany*, you've been quoting Shakespeare. Same goes for the phrases *forever and a day, heart of gold, in a pickle, one fell swoop*, and a *charmed life*.

Few hard facts are known about Shakespeare's life and habits, but based on the sheer volume of his works, it's not difficult to imagine that he was almost constantly writing—and probably thinking about writing when he wasn't. It might even be possible that he carried around a notebook like this one, so that he was prepared whenever and wherever inspiration struck. And if he didn't, well then, perhaps that would explain the line "My dull brain was wrought with things forgotten," in which Macbeth is preoccupied with trying to remember things he's forgotten.

Get ready to stop forgetting, harness the power of the Bard's words, and become a creative dynamo yourself. In the pages of this delightful notebook, you'll find some of Shakespeare's greatest and most memorable quotations that are sure to shift your imagination and motivation into high gear, including "This above all: to thine own self be true" and "Suit the action to the word, the word to the action" (both from *Hamlet*). Whether you're sketching your surroundings, crafting a poem, writing about your day, your dreams, your aspirations, or merely jotting down a to-do list, inspiration and wisdom from one of the world's greatest minds await every turn of the page.

There's no better time to dive in than now. In a moment of frustration, King Lear tells one of his daughters, "Nothing can come of nothing." Were any truer words ever spoken? Write it, sketch it, jot it, or whatever you like—just let your imagination fill these pages. After all, as the Bard himself observed in *As You Like It*: "The best is yet to do." And you never know—perhaps you'll even come up with a few new words or phrases along the way, too!

A NOTE FROM
THE PUBLISHER

To the Imaginitive Dreamer,
Doodler, or Aspiring Playwright:

 his elegant notebook pays tribute to
William Shakespeare with more than just
beautifully typeset presentations of his
most celebrated words. We've also curated a collection of ornate artwork created by illustrator Walter
Crane (1845–1915) for *The Tempest* and *Two
Gentleman of Verona*, which you'll find sprinkled
through the pages of your *Shakespeare Notebook*.
The artwork of this influential English illustrator
has graced special editions of the works of such
iconic writers as Edmund Spenser, Oscar Wilde, and
even Miguel de Cervantes. We're delighted to showcase a selection of the wonderful pieces that Crane
created to complement the Bard's words. We hope
these illustrious illustrations will inspire your artistic creativity, as well as your literary imagination!

Happy scribbling!

THURIO. "How now, Sir Proteus, are you crept before us?"

Sc: IV. 2.

I'LL CALL FOR
PEN & INK,
AND WRITE MY MIND.

Henry VI, Part I

VALENTINE. "Ruffian, let go that rude uncivil touch;
Thou friend of an ill fashion!"   Act V. 4.

O FOR A MUSE OF FIRE, THAT WOULD ASCEND THE BRIGHTEST HEAVEN OF INVENTION.

Henry V

PROS: BY ACCIDENT MOST STRANGE, BOUNTIFUL FORTUNE,
PERO NOW MY DEAR LADY, HATH MINE ENEMIES
BROUGHT TO THIS SHORE; ——

THIS ABOVE ALL:

TO THINE OWN SELF BE TRUE.

 HAMLET

NOTHING
WILL COME OF
NOTHING.

King Lear

SILVIA: "Go give your master this: tell him from me,
One Julia, that his changing thoughts forget,
Would better fit his chamber than this shadow." (Act IV)

**TO BE A WELL-FAVORED MAN
IS THE GIFT OF FORTUNE; BUT**

TO WRITE AND
READ COMES
BY NATURE.

❧ *Much Ado About Nothing* ❧

BOATSWAIN: "HENCE! WHAT CARE THESE
ROARERS FOR THE NAME OF KING?"

OUR DOUBTS
ARE TRAITORS
AND MAKE US
LOSE THE GOOD
WE OFT MIGHT WIN
BY FEARING TO
ATTEMPT.

MEASURE FOR MEASURE

AND SO,

FROM HOUR TO HOUR,

WE RIPE AND RIPE,

AND THEN,

FROM HOUR TO HOUR,

WE ROT AND ROT,

AND THEREBY

HANGS A TALE.

As You Like It

PROTEUS. "All happiness bechance to thee in Milan!"
VALENTINE. As much to you at home! and so, farewell.

Act I   Sc. 1

THINGS WON ARE DONE;
JOY'S SOUL
LIES IN THE DOING.

Troilus and Cressida

JULIA. "To Julia,"—Say, from whom? } Act 1
LUCETTA. That the contents will show. } Sc. 2

ENFORCE ATTENTION LIKE

DEEP HARMONY:

WHERE WORDS ARE SCARCE,

THEY ARE SELDOM

SPENT IN VAIN.

RICHARD II

**AND SINCE YOU CANNOT
SEE YOURSELF,
SO WELL AS BY REFLECTION,
I, YOUR GLASS, WILL MODESTLY
DISCOVER
TO YOURSELF,
THAT OF YOURSELF WHICH
YOU YET KNOW NOT OF.**

JULIUS CAESAR

CALIBAN:— AS·I·TOLD·THEE·BEFORE·I·AM·
SUBJECT·TO·A·TYRANT:·A·SORCERER— (ACT III)

AND AS

IMAGINATION
BODIES FORTH

THE FORMS OF

THINGS UNKNOWN,

THE POET'S PEN

TURNS THEM TO

SHAPES

AND GIVES TO AIRY NOTHING

A LOCAL HABITATION

AND A NAME.

A MIDSUMMER NIGHT'S DREAM

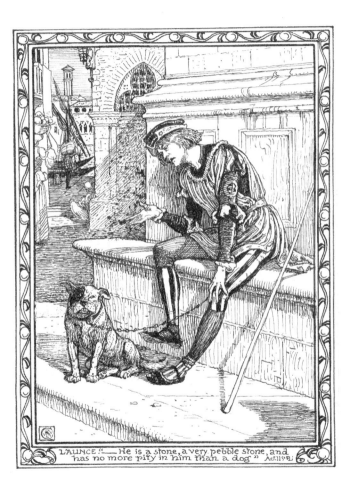

LAUNCE:"——— He is a stone, a very pebble stone, and
has no more pity in him than a dog" Act II Sc 2.

WHERE ART THOU, MUSE,

THAT THOU FORGET'ST SO LONG TO SPEAK OF THAT WHICH GIVES THEE

ALL THY MIGHT?

❧ "SONNET C" ❧

SUIT THE ACTION TO THE

WORD,

THE WORD TO THE

ACTION.

HAMLET

MIRANDA. SWEET LORD YOU PLAY ME FALSE.
FERDINAND. NO MY DEAREST LOVE
I WOULD NOT FOR THE WORLD. ACT V. SC. 1

THEY ARE

THE BOOKS, THE ARTS,
THE ACADEMES, THAT
SHOW, CONTAIN, AND

NOURISH

ALL THE WORLD.

Love's Labor's Lost

VALENTINE. "Welcome, dear Proteus! Mistress, I beseech you confirm his welcome with some special favour." 14

OH WONDERFUL, WONDERFUL,
AND MOST
WONDERFUL
WONDERFUL!

As You Like It

THIS IS
THE SHORT
AND
THE LONG
OF IT.

THE MERRY WIVES OF WINDSOR

About Cider Mill Press Book Publishers

Good ideas ripen with time. From seed to harvest, Cider Mill Press brings fine reading, information, and entertainment together between the covers of its creatively crafted books. Our Cider Mill bears fruit twice a year, publishing a new crop of titles each spring and fall.

Visit us on the web at

www.cidermillpress.com

or write to us at

12 Spring Street

PO Box 454

Kennebunkport, Maine 04046

The GLOBE PLAYHOUSE

1599–1613

A Conjectural Reconstruction by

C. Walter Hodges

KEY

AA	Main entrance
B	The Yard, where the 'groundlings' stood (for one penny admission)
CC	Entrances to lowest gallery (on payment of another penny)
D	Entrances at staircase and upper galleries
E	Corridor serving the different sections of the middle gallery
F	Middle gallery. (The 'Twopenny Rooms')
F G H J	'Gentlemen's Rooms' or 'Lords' Rooms'
J	The stage
K	The hangings being put up round the stage, (n.b. In some theatres this was boarded in)
L	The 'Hell' under the stage
M M	The stage trap, leading down to the Hell
N	Stage doors, leading into the tiring-house
	Curtained 'place behind the stage', sometimes opened for special scenes
O	Gallery above the stage, used as required sometimes by musicians, sometimes by spectators, and often as part of the play (e.g. Romeo and Juliet)
P	Backstage area (the tiring-house)
Q	Tiring-house door
R	Dressing rooms
S	Wardrobe and storage
T	The hut housing the machine for lowering enthroned gods, etc., to the stage
U	The 'Heavens'
W	Hoisting the playhouse flag

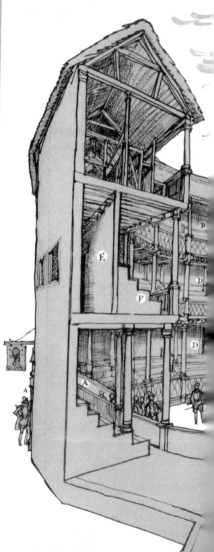